The Walking Logo

The Walking Logo

Taking Back My Life!

Volume 2

Carlos M. Christian

© 2017 Carlos M. Christian
All rights reserved.

ISBN: 1975983106
ISBN-13: 9781975983109

Table of Contents

   Introduction · vii
1. The Returning Citizen · 1
2. Take Back My Life · 6
3. Freedom Is Not Free · 12
4. Establish Ground · 15
5. Pick Your Friends and Your Family like You Pick Your Fruit · · · · · · · · 21
6. For Better or for Worse · 31
7. Financial Freedom · 37
8. The Speed of Recovery · 47
9. The Greatest Responsibility · 51

   Conclusion · 57

Introduction

THE OPPORTUNITY OF a lifetime presented itself, and you have the opportunity to walk out of hell, as you've so desperately wanted from the moment you realized that it was hell and conflicted with the desires of your spirit. Your out date is here. Your family awaits you at the gates, and you are ready to enjoy life on a whole different level from what you have grown used to during your recent stint in prison.

You've wanted to be productive and to be an asset to your family since day one, but you didn't have the information you needed to make good decisions. So you were incarcerated, but now you have another crack at doing it right.

Some people don't get released or, even worse, do not go to prison at all because of their untimely deaths—a result of the games in which they were involved. The majority of people who are incarcerated are released at some point, but few are able to take advantage of that opportunity. Seven out of ten people released from prison are reincarcerated within five years. The majority are incarcerated within the first year of their release.

Nobody who gets released from prison makes a declaration to return for more time because the institution treated him or her so well. These people return because of their inability to transition back into society. I've heard people attempt to explain why. Some say prisoners are in love with going to prison, and that is where they desire to rest their heads. They believe that those individuals see life as being easier when they are incarcerated. This is far from the truth. A person might accept prison, but I have never run across anyone who desired it.

CARLOS M. CHRISTIAN

The prison population has expanded tremendously since 1970, causing more people to need assistance to successfully transition back into society. In the past this did not drive the conversation, because the number of people affected was so low. Now with prisons in the United States costing taxpayers $80 billion per year, there is emphasis on making sure the people who get released from prison do not return.

In 2007, when I was twenty-nine years old, I was released from serving a ten-year sentence at Marion Correctional Institution in Marion, Ohio. I have officially been out of prison for ten years. During that time I have faced a slew of challenges, but I have been able to overcome them and continue to defy the odds. Statistically speaking, I should have been reincarcerated by now, but instead I am able to say that life is looking as I envisioned it when I was trapped in the penal system, hoping to go home. I had to overcome the mentality that gets so many people incarcerated.

I was incarcerated for attempted murder, possession of drugs, drug trafficking, and possession of firearms, so I knew the upstanding citizens of society wouldn't accept me easily. I knew the underworld would embrace me with open arms, which resulted in my incarceration in the first place. I had to overcome the temptation of falling back in line with my old associates, making money by selling drugs. I knew what that would result in. I understood this before my release, but faced with the dilemma of providing for my family, sometimes that understanding can be difficult to support. This is how so many people fall back into their old lifestyles.

I was surrounded by some good people who helped me adjust in society and offered me opportunities that aided my journey in staying out of prison. I secured stable employment and established a positive relationship with my children to be an influence in their lives so they could grow up and become successful adults. I was able to establish my credit, make investments, and budget my minimum-wage job to get to the next level. I have been to the Bahamas on family cruises six different times, just living life in a desirable way.

My former wife and I cofounded a nonprofit organization, the Starts Within Organization (SWO), which focuses on preparing people to

THE WALKING LOGO

successfully transition back into society before they are released from prison. SWO has touched thousands of individuals in the prison setting within the state of Ohio. I currently do this full time as my occupation, but I like to call it my assignment. I have the ability to give people the game on how to transition back into society and get the results I know they want. Being able to talk to people in society to get them to support the initiative of turning the penitentiary on its head and standing the community on its feet is fulfilling, to say the least. Making presentations in prisons to get the incarcerated to see opportunity where they usually cannot is also fulfilling.

The Walking Logo: Taking Back My Life is the follow-up to my first published book, *Prison Without Bars*, which discusses everything you need to know to be successful inside prison in order to build the foundation for success after your release.

I wrote *The Walking Logo: Taking Back My Life* to give individuals the keys to successfully transition back into society and live life at a high level and also to give individuals who are stagnant in society the proper information to progress. The only thing that separates the successful from the unsuccessful is access to information that influences their thinking and controls their behavior.

I know people who came home wanting to do the right thing, but because they didn't have the right information, they lasted only a few weeks before the demands of life outside prison became too overwhelming. They began to sell drugs and do everything that had gotten them incarcerated. They are now on the right track, but they admit that if they'd had the information then, they would never have lapsed. *The Walking Logo* provides the information they were missing.

The Walking Logo gives you the blueprint to get control of your life versus your life having control over you. The worst way to wake up every day is to know that life will drag you wherever it deems necessary.

In *Prison Without Bars*, I wrote that I became free while I was incarcerated in order to maintain my freedom once I was released. So although I was in prison, I did what I had to do to eliminate the bars from my mind that kept me restricted. Prison of the mind is the worst incarceration that you can face.

CARLOS M. CHRISTIAN

The Walking Logo combats the prison in which so many people reside within their own minds, even though they are free from an actual facility. Not knowing how to function in society is the main factor behind incarceration.

Everybody needs to understand how to earn credit, how to establish themselves in the courts with their children, how to budget, and how to know the difference between nurturing relationships and toxic relationships. Not knowing puts you in one of two categories: either you are on your way to prison or you are on your way back to prison, if you don't get murdered first—or maybe you are in prison, but without the bars!

I faced many challenges in getting control of my life, but those are not as complicated when you have the information to overcome them. Next-level living is derived from next-level thinking, and you can't think on the next level if you don't have the information to do so. If you were trying to start a business, and Bill Gates, whose business savvy made him a billionaire, walked into the room, you would be a fool not to want to pick his brain. I have been able to go from selling drugs at thirteen and doing a ten-year prison sentence to successfully transitioning back into society and assisting others to do the same. I am officially the Bill Gates of reentry!

1

The Returning Citizen

THE ATTENTION THE returning citizen receives is now at an all-time high because of media publicity and activists who are fighting against mass incarceration. A report by the Pew Charitable Trust found that of the 2.3 million people who are incarcerated in the United States, 1.2 million are parents of minors. That means 2.7 million children have a parent in jail or prison in the United States. This topic has even become a part of *Sesame Street*, with the introduction of a character by the name of Alex, who has an incarcerated parent.

We are in a time when people who are incarcerated want to be released, and people who are in society want them to be released. Every year 650,000 individuals across the United States return to their communities from prisons. Of people who are incarcerated, 95 percent will be released back into society. There is a push to release nonviolent offenders before their slated times of release. Documentaries such as *13^(TH)*, a featured show on Netflix that brought awareness to the boom in prison populations, demonstrate that society is up in arms about getting people out of prison and back to their families.

Government agencies and nonprofit organizations get funding to aid individuals once they are released from prison. The possibility of the returning citizen becoming successful is greater than it was thirty years ago, when incarceration was not such a common topic. Now celebrities get incarcerated and released from prison and jails at a higher rate. All of this brings awareness of this issue to the masses, which only helps society receive the returning citizen.

As a person who successfully transitioned back into society, I am excited about the opportunity that lies in wait for the returning citizen getting released from prison. After the 2016 election that left Donald Trump standing victorious as the president-elect, it is feasible that in the future, the president of the United States could very well be an individual who was once incarcerated and has turned his or her life around to become a productive citizen. Anything is possible!

Even with many people—especially families—pulling for released individuals to be successful, the opportunity is often squandered, and the former prisoners usually return to the lives they grew accustomed to.

If you were not an auto mechanic and did not have the knowledge to work on cars, and I asked you to change my oil or repair my brakes, you would not be able to do it. If I told an actual auto mechanic to perform one of those tasks, he or she would be able to get it done rather quickly. Although both of you are *aware* of oil changes and brakes on a vehicle, only one of you has the specialized knowledge to perform the task. If the mechanic taught you, you would also be able to perform that task, because you would know which tools to use and what bolts to loosen in order to get the job done.

The majority of individuals who are incarcerated do not get the information relevant to sustaining a life in regular society upon release. They may take programming, but the programming does not prepare them for what they are going to see once they are released. Nobody wants to see the program certificates that prisoners have completed during their prison stints. Although they are released and want to capitalize on the opportunity and make a life in their new world, not having the information makes that next to impossible. They don't know how to navigate the child-support system, conduct positive interviews, or go about establishing their credit. They don't have the information about what it takes to establish positive relationships with people outside of the person they were before and during incarceration. They aren't even aware of the importance of opening a checking account.

People underestimate the power of knowledge and what it can do to people's psyches once they obtain it. The reason people lack motivation is that they lack direction. People need direction to successfully return to society from prison; this will motivate them to battle the temptations they will face that could lead them into recidivism. When individuals are released with seventy-five dollars and a tight sweat suit with a windbreaker, and somebody tells them the steps they have to take to be successful, it usually goes in one ear and out the other. They cannot relate to that information. So they disregard it and go to the people they know and trust, but unfortunately, those are the ones who will ultimately keep them going through the revolving door that leads to prison.

I have spoken to men released from prison who said they were ready to do everything they needed to do to be successful in society, but the available support was not the type they actually needed. Agencies have their ideas of what the returning citizen needs to be successful, and those ideas are simple at best. Good-hearted people say, "We'll have a place for them to come and eat when they're hungry." If they were making money before they got incarcerated, giving them food will not inspire them to not relapse into their old lifestyle. The belief that the returning citizen is looking for a handout is one of the greatest misconceptions that I have come across. Their whole existence has been based on making it happen on their own.

The greater challenge is to get the returning citizen to accept the assistance that people offer versus depending on the assistance to help them change their situations around. "Free" is not the key word to motivate the returning citizen to stay on the right track to success. That word, "free," is not direction.

Despite the desires on both sides for the individual to be successful, a disconnect remains that precludes it from happening, and seven out of ten people who are released from prison fall to recidivism within five years in the United States. Recidivism means a relapse into criminal behavior, often after a sanction or some form of intervention.

The recidivism rate is calculated based on the number of people who have committed another crime or who have violated their parole and conditions of release. This is where the numbers can lie because they do not calculate the individuals who were released from prison and were murdered because they relapsed into their old behaviors.

The ultimate goal has to be to prevent the returning citizens from going back into the behavior that got them incarcerated in the first place. It is not OK if they go back into that behavior but don't increase the recidivism rate, because they are killed or aren't caught for their crimes. The families will still be broken, producing more adults like the ones taxpayers are tired of paying for. The incarcerated population will continue to increase.

Returning citizens are too valuable to the community and to society for us to not put our all into ensuring that they have everything they need to be successful upon release. The key thing they need is direction!

There can be no more of the classes currently offered to them, where they attend for a week and get a hundred dollars, with the expectation that they will maintain a mentality that is contradictory to prison. The programs with incentives such as gift cards and stipends do not seriously influence returning citizens to abandon the mentality that got them incarcerated, although they do provide good information that can take them to another level. The returning citizens consider where they will truly be after the gift cards, stipends, and allocated grant dollars evaporate.

The grant dollars are driven by numbers more than actual results, so sometimes the focus can be as well. I touched on the point earlier that numbers can lie. People may go through the reentry program offered by a community agency funded by grant dollars without being truly affected by the program and then go back to doing what they were doing before they got incarcerated. When this happens, those grant dollars are squandered and did not accomplish anything but a nice report about the people who completed the class to present to the funding agency. The community is still at a disadvantage because the same individuals are operating from the same bad information, and they are feeding it to the people in their families and neighborhoods whom they continue to influence.

I advocate doing away with filling these salaried positions strictly with people who went to college to learn about the returning citizen but never went through the process and don't know what it is like. The best prospective

THE WALKING LOGO

candidates for key positions in organizations that assist the newly released are people who have actually returned to society and who also possess the required technical knowledge. One cannot transfer information if it is not an established relationship. The returning citizen has to be able to relate to the person giving advice on what it takes to be successful and how important it is.

In Ohio, we use the term "restored citizen" for someone who has returned to society and is now restored as an asset to the community. Restored citizens have abandoned the old mentality that got them into trouble and embraced a new, positive mentality. We need restored citizens in these agencies to be the ones meeting those who are released from prison.

If those who offer assistance were once in that position, that establishes the direction the returning citizens need in order to be motivated to evolve. They can begin to see themselves not working at minimum-wage jobs for all their lives to stay out of prison, but working until they can go to the next level and eventually have the ability to do something they enjoy for a living.

With the Starts Within Organization, the company I cofounded in 2011, I make it clear that the people who fill the positions in the organization are people who have actually applied the information and were disciplined enough to evolve into assets in their community. The program manager is someone who was incarcerated and has the ability to connect with the population, and that is easily a position that earns $70,000 a year. We are not programming to get numbers to get more grants. We are programming to make an impact and provide the information that changes a mind-set. That position and other positions are not given—they are earned.

Although I would love everybody to get on board and do what needs to be done to evolve into individuals who will be assets to the movement of turning the penitentiary on its head and standing the community on its feet, I understand that some people just won't be ready to change and do what needs to be done to stay out of prison. The people who will be successful are those who are able to see the opportunity to improve themselves, take on a civilian mentality, and abandon the outlaw mentality. This will be scary, but it will be mandatory. The programming offered upon release has to be programming that helps accomplish this.

2

Take Back My Life

I RECALL LOOKING UP the aisle at night when the majority of people were asleep in a dormitory of about 120 people. I would zone out and wonder whether this would ever be over. Would I ever go home?

I was incarcerated when I was nineteen years old, and all of my twenties were spent in that hell. I started having those thoughts around the seven-year mark, after I had filed for early release and been denied by the judge three times. I had a positive institutional record, and my heart was sincerely in the right place to go home and be a father to my son, who was seven years old.

I had witnessed so many people who were released from prison only to be right back within a few months. I knew that I would capitalize on the opportunity of freedom once it was given to me.

The day finally came, and I was released from prison in February 2007, when the country was entering the Great Recession. I was given a furlough to a halfway house in Cleveland, Ohio, to complete the last six months of my sentence. A halfway house is designed to ease individuals back into society, with the halfway house still providing structure. This was critical to me because while I was seeking employment, I wasn't burdened with paying bills, and I would be able to build a nice foundation to really take flight. I would be able to go out and get employment and ride public transportation during my allotted time. If you don't follow the rules of the halfway house, then you are sent back to prison to complete the remainder of your sentence. The money you earned from working had to be turned over to the halfway house, where they would put it into an account. They would calculate 25 percent of your gross and deduct it from your net.

I was excited to be able to witness regular society. The first day I arrived at the facility, I told my brothers that I was there, and others from the neighborhood also found out that I was there. I was gone for nine and a half years, and people were ecstatic about me coming home.

When you get released, it's like everybody wants to see you, like a newly released and highly sought-out movie that just hit the theaters. When you are incarcerated, it can seem that the love is not there because of the limited contact with the people on the streets. Nobody comes to visit or writes you letters to stay in contact.

My brothers came to see me at the halfway house immediately and brought me some clothes so I wouldn't have to wear what I had from prison. I had not worn jeans or a regular shirt in years. People brought me expensive Air Jordans and leather coats so I would be able to survive the Cleveland winter. This support was beneficial to me in transitioning back into society after so long. When you are released from a long prison sentence, you usually do not have anything left, and you have to start over, so having that assistance was instrumental.

It was all surreal to me at the time. The fact that America was going through its worst economic hit since the Great Depression did not register with me at all. I was free, and I was ready to make it happen. I would have to go through orientation for a week, and then I would be able to go job hunting and score a job. I was ready to go, get it done, and defy the odds of the returning citizen. If seven out of ten return to prison within a five-year period, then I would be among those three who didn't. I was focused and so convinced that prison was hell that I could not see myself giving up the opportunity of freedom for anybody or anything.

I believed I had a lot going for me from an educational point of view, and that would be beneficial for me in obtaining employment. I was optimistic about my success in getting employed. In my mind, getting employment was imperative in taking my life back. It was necessary, and I was determined.

That determination did not land me a job initially. I went everywhere trying to get hired, including the dreaded fast-food restaurants, which is a big deal for someone who used to make money selling drugs. I was desperate, and it didn't matter as long as it was employment. I had a list of employers who said they hire returning citizens, but it was outdated and inaccurate. I was putting my effort into getting employment while I was permitted the time to go to interviews and fill out applications, but I got nowhere.

My good friend, whom I consider my brother, took me to these jobs to fill out applications and do interviews, and he said, "Dang, Los, I am getting exhausted watching you fill out all these applications…it's like you are a professional application filler-outer."

I was getting discouraged because the main thing that came up was the attempted-murder conviction on my record. The greatest challenges in transitioning were keeping my mind in a positive place and continuing to push forward and place my applications with other employers. I had to tell myself that if nine told me no, then the tenth would tell me yes.

I had some close friends who made names for themselves in the streets. All I had to do was say the word, and I could have gotten a package immediately to get back on my feet. I just did not see selling drugs as a way to get on my feet, so I wasn't even tempted by that option.

Other people in the halfway house were having some of the same issues with employment, but instead of fighting them, they succumbed to the temptation of making money their old ways, and they began to sell drugs during the time allotted to them to look for employment. Usually this decision would get them returned to prison.

I stayed the course and continued to work with the staff in the halfway house and took the programming they suggested to better my chances of getting employment, although I already knew the information they were teaching. It clicked that the best chance I had at getting employment was to get a referral from a respected professional in this new world I was trying to enter. I started to connect with people in the facility who were in charge of employment and getting leads for clients. The employment specialist took such a liking to my determination and positive attitude that he referred me to one of his close friends who was an employer. He usually didn't refer people because he didn't want to jeopardize their relationship for someone who wasn't serious, but he read me as being serious, so he presented me with the opportunity.

I took advantage of it, and I was hired full-time. Although the job paid only six dollars and eighty-five cents an hour, I worked it like it was for forty dollars an hour. In my mind, I came from twenty-two cents an hour, so I was on a 600 percent raise. Plus I was building my work history to continue to evolve as a civilian and move further away from being an outlaw. I had to look at the positive in every situation in order to treat it as positive.

I had full-time employment two weeks after I was released from prison, and I was feeling optimistic about the direction of my life. Shortly after, I was granted my first weekend pass. A weekend pass allows you to go to an approved family member's address for the weekend when you don't have to work at your job. I would officially show my face to people who had not seen me in a decade.

I was excited to see the old neighborhood. Seeing and being around people you grew up with…all of that love can be intoxicating after prison, where people don't celebrate you. They tolerate you at best. It was like I'd been dead and was resurrected, and everybody was appreciative to have me back alive.

I was especially excited to be able to spend some time with some old girlfriends. After being in prison for ten years, being touched by another human being in a romantic way was foreign to me, and I missed it dearly. I had yearned to be next to someone soft, so when I got the opportunity, I truly felt like I was living again.

I got with some of my old friends, and we had a few drinks to celebrate my being home, but I didn't get too tipsy. I understood that I had to report back to the halfway house when the weekend was over, and I didn't want to have alcohol in my system. The fellas understood and supported my decision.

The splash of freedom was no joke. The struggle is reporting back to the halfway house, because you don't want the good times to stop. I reported back on time because I knew that this was one step closer to being able to enjoy my freedom fully. I wasn't going to step over a dollar bill and pick up a dime because it was shiny. Skipping out on the weekend and not reporting back to the halfway house was picking up the dime. I would have more fun temporarily, but that would come crashing down once they revoked my pass and sent me back to prison. Picking up the dollar bill was doing what needed to be done in the halfway house so I didn't have to go to prison or any institution again.

I saw guys who didn't turn in their checks because they felt that giving the halfway house 25 percent of their earnings was too much, and they willingly embraced the consequence of getting sent back to prison. They kept that whole check one time and then wouldn't have the opportunity to make any more money, because they were back in prison for the rest of their sentences. They felt like they were getting hustled, and they responded based on their feelings. Anytime that you allow your feelings to control your behavior, your life will be unstable. When you are transitioning from prison back into society, you must spend the majority of your time stabilizing your foundation and not compromising it. The only way you can do that is to operate through your mind and not your feelings. Your mind is the most powerful tool you have, and it will determine where you will be in life. It will determine whether you will be a success or a recidivist.

I had to continue to tell myself the things that would keep me on track, because the way I felt sometimes was not productive. One day my supervisor called me into the office after the end of work, and he told me that that it was my last day because business was too slow, and he could not justify keeping me there even though I was a great employee. I was the last one in, so I was the first one out is how he said he made the decision.

When you are trying to do right and you get an undesirable result, it takes a strong mind because it is so tempting to respond out of your feelings and find yourself in a situation that you don't want. If you don't like the bad, then you will definitely not like the worse. The decisions you make during bad times will determine whether those bad times will become worse or better. This is life, and you must deal with it.

The bus ride back to the halfway house was the longest I'd had in a while. I was hurt because I had really started to get the hang of the job and was doing well, and now I was back to square one.

THE WALKING LOGO

I stayed the course and worked on my relationships, and I got employed at a few more jobs while I was at the halfway house because other case managers referred me. They took me to be a quality individual whom they didn't mind sticking their necks out to help.

After successfully completing my time at the halfway house, I was sentenced to serve five years of post-release control. Post-release control (PRC) is a period of supervision of an offender by the Adult Parole Authority following release from imprisonment. It includes one or more post-release control sanctions imposed by the Parole Board, pursuant to Ohio Revised Code (ORC) section 2967.28. Post-release control applies to offenders whose crimes were committed on or after July 1, 1996, and who were sentenced under Senate Bill 2 to a definite prison term. For some offenders, the ORC mandates post-release control. For others, the ORC specifies that post-release control is discretionary by the Parole Board. Although I was due to serve five years PRC, I was cut loose after two because I was doing everything that I needed to in the eyes of my probation officer.

I have been out of the halfway house for ten years now, and I have faced a variety of challenges, including child support wiping out my checking account because I was behind in payments after I was fired from my job. One thing that remained constant was my determination to not be a recidivist. It is not an easy feat to overcome prison and transition back into society successfully, but with the right people in your corner giving you the right guidance, it is definitely possible to defy the odds.

I am now divorced from my second son's mother, who was my girlfriend when I was first released, but we still have a positive relationship, and we positively coparent our son together. He stays with me throughout the week, and he goes to his mother's house on the weekend. I have the joy of running the Starts Within Organization and truly fulfilling my purpose. Taking my life back was the best decision I could've made because I honestly like my existence on this earth while it is in my hands versus the hands of the system.

3

Freedom Is Not Free

JUST BECAUSE FREEDOM includes the word "free" doesn't mean that it comes without cost. The greatest misunderstanding that people who get released from prison have is that freedom is free. You must continue to pay a price to be able to truly experience real freedom.

The Walking Logo backs the ideology that freedom is bought with a string of good decisions. The only way that you can make good decisions is with the right information. If you do not know how to eat at the table because you don't have the proper information to do so, then it would be ridiculous to expect you to have good table etiquette. Maybe you skip over the silverware and eat the food with your hands, barbarian-style. We can blame your behavior on you not knowing and not having the proper information to make a good decision while at the table.

Men and women get released from prison and become recidivists because of their inability to adapt to a society that is completely opposite of the one they have known for the majority of their lives. People will stay in a known hell for fear of a strange heaven. They will continue to live the same life regardless of knowing how the story ends because at least they are comfortable and know how to live it; they have the information that fits the lifestyle. Nobody is OK with the consequences of embracing the known hell, but they simply do not have enough information about the

THE WALKING LOGO

strange heaven to make it less strange, more familiar, and more possible to obtain.

The Walking Logo will cover six areas that are needed to be successful and take possession of your life. The main key to living a fulfilled life is that if you do not manage your life, then someone will manage it for you, and in doing so will benefit him- or herself more than you. That is the payment for not properly managing your life. Whatever you choose, your life will not go unmanaged. It would serve you best to do it yourself.

The first area of focus that we will discuss in *The Walking Logo* is establishing ground. If your foundation is built on shaky ground, it is nearly impossible to be successful. What you do within your first year of release will dictate the likelihood of you making a successful transition back into society and not returning to prison. This is when most people who get released set up their direction to go back into prison or live the life that they were destined to live.

The second area of focus will be picking your friends. You are guilty by association. It is one of the most challenging areas, and many people fall short because they don't have the ability to identify toxic relationships versus nurturing relationships. Some relationships are toxic because they are not adding value to your life. It is a must that you identify which is which.

The third area of focus will be obtaining financial freedom. The lack of money is one of the main reasons why people commit crimes in the first place. *The Walking Logo* will cover how to establish credit, the importance of purchasing a home, budgeting, investing in the stock market, and building your assets.

The fourth area of focus will be choosing your significant other. *The Walking Logo* will discuss the importance of not rushing your decision to settle down too quickly without having all the information to make a quality decision on such an important part of your success.

The fifth area of focus in *The Walking Logo* is establishing yourself in the lives of your children. We will discuss how to eliminate the barriers that can prevent you from being the best parent that you desire to be. The barriers we will discuss can come in the form of child support or a controlling coparent who may prevent you from seeing your children. A positive relationship with your children can be the foundation of remaining successful after prison.

The final area of focus will be doing what you need to do to protect your environment. The onus will be on you to ensure that you can be most productive in your environment and that it gets you to be the best you.

People do not succeed after prison, because they lack information that inspires and motivates them to do what needs to be done to be successful. The greatest obstacle you face is figuring out how to embrace a new way of living that is different from the one that got you imprisoned. As a returning citizen, you must be able to take advantage of the opportunities offered that do not put you in adverse conditions but rather in desirable conditions.

Sometimes during this walk, you will have to embrace your shadows and walk alone, but it will be worth making that temporary sacrifice. The new you will not fit in with your old crew, but don't be discouraged. This is the path to greatness.

Another obstacle will be the distractions of the world. It will be tempting to just party when you get released, because everybody wants to spend time with you and resources on you. This can lead to you falling into a full-time party mode and not building your foundation in a solid manner.

The best way to overcome the obstacles is to really be connected to positive circles. These will be your greatest assets once you are released. A positive circle can be full of employees, since you want to become an employee as well. The people you hang around will either feed your mind that it is possible to continue to evolve into a person who is not reduced to prison time or getting killed on the street corner somewhere, or they'll tell you that it is impossible to change and that life has dealt you a bad hand that you have to play and lose.

This transition will truly take the guidance of people who have been able to successfully transition back into society. *The Walking Logo* will serve as the guidance you need to be successful. Once you understand that you are more valuable in your household with your children and living life in a way that fits you, you can learn everything else about how society works and make the adjustment. A person who was once a liability in the community and then became an asset in the community is truly a blessing to the world. The work it takes to make that transformation is heavy, but the reward is great.

4

Establish Ground

THE FOUNDATION YOU lay within the first six months of your release will determine the success of your transition back into society and a life that is ideal. People approach me all the time and ask, "How have you been able to stay home?"

I always reply that it was the way I came out the gate. I was intent on being successful and not returning to the behavior that got me incarcerated. I knew what really mattered to me, and that was making sure I was there to raise my son, who was then ten years old. His mother told me he had gained fondness for things that are acquired in the streets. I was thirteen years old when I started selling crack and carrying guns, and that led me to my ten-year prison sentence. I was keyed to do what I needed to do to ensure my son did not go down that same path.

Laying my solid foundation was instrumental to my success. The first block was getting employment. This is one of the first things you need to do when you are released from prison. I hear all the talk about the difficulty in obtaining employment, but I have found the difficulty lies in people accepting the type of employment that is available to them at that particular time. I came out of the penitentiary with no hang-ups about what kind of job I got or what it paid. As long as the job didn't compromise my integrity, I was OK with taking it. I was starting at ground level, and I was confident I would build up if I got started.

You don't have to be great to get started, but you have to get started to be great. That twenty-dollars-an-hour job might not be available to you when you are first released. You still must get employed. I got my first credit card from that minimum-wage job. I purchased my first house from the time spent at that low-paying job, when I needed to provide two years' work history to solidify the mortgage from the bank. I was working hard-labor jobs for eight dollars an hour, but I worked them knowing they would get me established in my new life. Employment brings value that is necessary for the psyche.

Returning citizens who recidivate usually say they are trying to take it slow and get accustomed to society. You do not have that time because you are playing from behind, and your movements have to reflect that. I was gone for ten years. I did not feel I had time to waste or any margin for error.

It will be difficult to take the jobs you are offered, but everything is controlled by the way you think. The only way the job will work for you is if you make it work in your mind. I was working sixty-hour weeks doing metal framing in Cleveland. The overtime was plentiful because of the demand of the business and the low wages. Working sixty-hour workweeks was critical for me to stay busy when I was first released. The worst thing that a returning citizen can have is an idle mind, commonly known as the devil's playground.

Either I was working or I was getting some rest to go into work. If it had not been for the job's demands on my time, I could have easily fallen back into the streets. When the weekend came, I went to see some of the friends I had known growing up, and we drank and cracked jokes. The demands of the job kept that to a minimum. My time was accounted for, so the time I had for the things that would not get me to a better place was limited. When you do not have anywhere to be, then it's easy to fall back in with the old crew simply because of the love that is there. I was taking positive steps toward being successful because I was making progress. I was gaining work history, making money, and not doing something that would put me back into prison.

Being in the halfway house gave me the ability to get my legs underneath me. During my time there, I was able to work and save my money. When I was released, I had a job as well as $3,500 in savings from the jobs I had worked while I was there.

THE WALKING LOGO

The exact day I was released from the halfway house, I had my first month's rent and security deposit ready for my own apartment. I didn't want to live with my father because I had been living with someone for ten years. I was ready to unlock the keys to my own doors. I made sure that the apartment was manageable with what I was making at my job. The apartment cost me $475 per month, and it was a one bedroom.

I was excited because my life was coming together. It wasn't coming together because I wanted it to, but because I expected it to, and you could tell by my approach to life when I was released. I was adamant about getting a job, and it didn't matter what I was getting paid, but I saw in my mind how it would be beneficial, and it didn't take long to be proven right. Having the ability to get an apartment was fulfilling as an adult. I say "as an adult" because when you are incarcerated, it's like you are stripped of your adulthood when it comes to managing your life.

The apartment was not the sexiest, but it was mine, and it was better than prison. Nothing says freedom more than paying bills! When you pay bills, you know you have a say in what is going on in your life. If I had stayed with somebody, I would have had to come in when they said and did what they said out of respect for their home. I personally had enough of operating like that, so the apartment was instrumental for me to take advantage of my freedom. The apartment had roaches, as should be expected when you get it for that price, but it was mine. I just told myself the roaches were paying some of the rent, and that is why I was able to get it for that price. It was their place just as much as it was mine. Nobody could tell me anything. I had my own keys and my own space.

If I had looked at other people who had been out and established themselves, it might have discouraged me about the progression of my life. One of the main things that you have to do once you are released from prison is stay focused on yourself. Looking at other people's situations and seeing where they are could cause you to not appreciate your accomplishments. My good friend was staying in a nice place in the suburbs on the lake. Although his house was nice, I thought my apartment was nice as well, compared to where I came from. If I had compared our houses without any other context, then that could have depressed me. Instead I focused on where I came from and asked myself whether I had progressed. Because the answer was yes, I was more appreciative of the accomplishment.

Losing appreciation is one of the first things that happens to people when they get released from prison. This is what causes them to disregard the opportunity and go back to the things that got them incarcerated in the first place. They lose focus on the beauty of freedom, although they yearned for it when they were incarcerated. In turn, they equate incarceration with freedom—that is, until they go back into the facility, and then they are back to yearning for freedom. It is important that you compare yourself to yourself.

The times when I was down about my situation were when I looked at other people and their positions in life and ignored where I came from and focused on where I was currently. That made me to want to speed up the process to get to where they were, and I had to reexamine myself and say that I was better than I was yesterday, so I was winning. It doesn't matter that my friend is winning when I am winning as well.

The problem comes when you feel like you are losing. I cannot lose if I continue to compete against myself. I came from rock bottom. How could I not win? Having a job paying eight dollars an hour was winning. Having my own apartment was winning. Having the say in when I wanted to work out was winning, and talking on the phone when I chose to was winning. I could go on and on about what made me believe that I was winning. If I believed that I was winning, then that is what came out in my behavior.

Winners carry themselves a certain way, and they are attractive to the masses. Winning is established in the mind before you can see it in real life. If you don't establish it in the mind, then nothing that is given to you and no opportunity presented to you will make you out to be a winner. You will still do what losers do, which is losing!

I had my job, and I had my furnished apartment on my first day out of the halfway house. I was ready to move on to my next building block in my foundation. I got my driver's license two days before my release from the halfway house so that when I did get a car, I would be legal. My mind operated in a way that encouraged me to play by the book and be all-the-way legit.

THE WALKING LOGO

When I was incarcerated, I listened to music in my headphones, just imagining myself rolling. Driving your own car is something that improves your quality of living.

I went to go look for a car on the second day that I was out, and I came to a place that tried to put me in a $10,000 car loan. I didn't have any credit, so they said they would take a cosigner. I rejected every bit of their so-called opportunity because I had $2,300 to pay for a car at most, not $10,000. I truly did not understand credit at that time, but I knew that being in a $10,000 car when I didn't have the money to cover it or the employment to justify it probably wouldn't end well. I didn't want to overextend myself and be worse off than when I started. I heard about people getting their cars repossessed because they couldn't pay the car note.

I figured that it would cost me more because I didn't have any established credit. I was OK with not being able to drive the $10,000 car because I understood that it wasn't me at that time. I knew that in time it would be, if I stayed disciplined.

I went to a place on West Sixty-Fifth and Clark in Cleveland, Ohio, and I found a 1995 Buick Regal two door for $1,750. I signed the paperwork and paid for the car in cash, and I was rolling like it was a $10,000 car. I cracked the seats back and blasted the music as loud as it could go. I was free, and it felt good.

Having my own transportation was another slice of heaven because depending on other people to take me places conflicted against my spirit. I didn't like my friend coming ten to fifteen minutes late every time to pick me up. I did not like getting caught in the rain at the bus stop, waiting for a bus that was a bit behind. The inconveniences were enough for me to rejoice in the 1995 Buick Regal like it was a Mercedes-Benz. Life was clicking for me.

I went immediately to the insurance company up the street, and I got the car insured. My license was suspended because I didn't have car insurance when I was seventeen years old. I would not make that mistake again at twenty-nine.

After I got everything squared away with my job, my housing, and my transportation, the next thing I had to do was meet my probation officer. As

CARLOS M. CHRISTIAN

I was on PRC, I had to check in with my PO to sign what I needed and to let him know where I was working and any other information that he needed. I was determined to do whatever I needed to so I could get off PRC before the standard five years.

He set it up for me to come and see him every other month. As I had a child-support order that was still active from when I was in prison, I didn't have to pay the supervision fee of twenty dollars every month, which was a plus. The returning citizen getting a violation is all too common, and I wanted to ensure that I knew what my probation officer expected of me so I could meet those expectations. I was not going to make up my own rules; I would follow the ones they gave me. I was determined to keep my life as simple as possible. I would color inside the lines so the picture would look like I desired it to look. I wanted a picture that didn't present a depiction of institutions or supervision by an agency. You must be serious about everything once you get released from prison to be able to make the transition.

I see people who don't take parole or probation seriously and get reincarcerated. I see people who don't take getting employment seriously enough and get reincarcerated. You must cross your t's and dot your i's to be successful after prison. The greatest mistake returning citizens make is believing they can relax and not be so serious. They get into a partying mind-set because everybody around them is encouraging the celebration. When you've been gone, everybody wants to buy you drinks, and women want to hang with you. It can be misleading to returning citizens. The reward is not getting released but rather staying released.

5

Pick Your Friends and Your Family like You Pick Your Fruit

THE WRONG CROWD can put you in a compromising situation, and you must be careful to identify who is who and what is what. Not all the people who say they are for you are really for you, and it is not intentional most of the time. It just is what it is. The reason they aren't for you is because they aren't truly for themselves. If they are not motivated to improve their lives, it will be difficult for them to be motivated to help you improve your life.

It's the difference between those who are attached to you and those who are connected to you. Those who are attached to you will drain you and leave you worse off than when they first came into your environment. These are the ones you have to keep at a distance. What makes this so difficult is that this can be your brother, cousin, best friend growing up, or even your parent. It doesn't matter what the relationship is—it is mandatory that you keep them at bay in order to achieve what so many fail to achieve, which is not recidivating.

Close friends told me that I was not the same anymore and that I treated them like I didn't have the time for them that I used to. All I could say was that my time was accounted for, and I could no longer sit around and get drunk and high all day, because that would put me into the mind-set to begin selling drugs again. How else could I support that lifestyle? The people who made that statement were still in the streets, so this is why they didn't understand about the time I had available.

People don't know how serious it is to do ten years in prison and not be around the people whom you love. I've had people say that the time flew by, but I had a different experience. It was hell for me, and I felt it every single day.

You run from the attachments and toward the people you make a connection with because they will help you overcome the challenges you face returning to society. The people you connect with will give you power; they will help you grow, and it will be good energy. This is needed in order to be successful in life, and not just when you're returning from prison. Picking your friends and family like your fruit is saying that you pick your fruit carefully. You have to do the same thing with the people you allow to dominate your time once you get released from prison. You can pick the friends you will be around, and you can also pick the family you will be around. That cousin might not be best for you to hang around, even though the two of you grew up more like siblings than cousins.

I was around people who had responsibilities because I knew that I had responsibilities as well. I was around people who were employed and had jobs to be at Monday through Friday. Since my goal at the time was to be an employee, it was best that I hung around employees so I could remain an employee. Opportunities come through relationships, and I got some great opportunities through people I met at my place of employment. When people went on to find better employment opportunities, they always reached out to let me know about the new opportunity. Some of the jobs I've had came from ex-coworkers going somewhere else and establishing a good relationship with the hiring supervisors, and then giving them my name. So I was able to get employed regardless of my having a felony. I was connected to their star employees, and that is all that needed to be said. I was hired based on their characters.

Hanging around people who are not where you want to be or going where you want to go will not get you there at all. They don't know the direction, nor are they interested in finding it. In order for you to be successful, you must keep those people at a distance, no matter if they are your family or your best friends from childhood. I know how difficult that can be, but it must be done. I would give them a little time because I didn't want to be standoffish, and I did love them, but that time was limited, and they knew it.

I connected with a brother named Mike at one of my jobs, and he was home for close to two years after doing seven years in a federal prison for selling drugs. He was convinced that prison was not his cup of tea, and he had been employed since he came home. He was instrumental in keeping me on my path to success. He was in the process of buying his house, and he used the minimum-wage job he got when he was released from prison as part of his two-year work history to secure his home loan. I never knew the process of getting a house, but seeing him do it let me know it was possible. He gave me a lot of game that I still benefit from today.

It is not what you put in somebody's hand that stays but what you put in somebody's head. What is in the hand can be lost, never to return, but what is put in the head can always keep something in your hand. Knowledge is powerful, and that brother turned me on to some heavy-duty knowledge that created opportunity in my mind. Mike was the first to teach me about the value of credit and how to use it in your favor. These are the types of connections that will take you to the next level. These connections are mandatory. It was great that he understood the streets and had a solid reputation, but he made the conscious choice to remove himself from that life and pursue a life that put him in places he desired. He was successful in my eyes, so I made sure that I picked his brain on the regular. I didn't have to act like life didn't matter around him in order to be cool, because we both understood that life was a blessing, and we were willing to do whatever needed to be done to experience it in a way that we desired.

When I first came home, I was hanging out a lot, and I had to remove myself from that crowd because I started to get too loose and the influence became too strong. People think they are strong enough to battle the influence, but I assure you that it is next to impossible. It is only a matter of time before you become like the people who dominate the majority of your time.

I was cautious of who was in my immediate circle. They had to be individuals who would help me overcome prison and the mentality that led me there in the first place. I put my all into those relationships because they would make the difference in my future.

> The wise man who built his house on the rock when the rain came down, the streams rose, and the winds blew and beat against that house; yet it did not fall, because it had its foundation on the rock. The foolish man who built his house on sand when the rain came down, the streams rose, and the winds blew and beat against that house, and it fell with a great crash.
> —Matthew 7:24–27

This is a powerful scripture, and it has a great meaning. When what you are standing on is not solid, then you will likely fall once trials and tribulations come to challenge you. One thing about life is that, regardless of whether you are just getting out of prison or have never been, it will still throw its challenges at you. If you are not grounded or don't stand for the right things, then it is difficult to continue your path to success. The reason you want to stay out of prison has to be strong enough in order for you to be successful in your transition.

People say all the time that they just need to get out of prison, but they truly don't have a strong enough reason why it would make a difference. Their reasons are primarily based on themselves and their current discomfort. If your reason for staying out of prison is not greater than yourself, then I would seriously suggest that you recheck your reason for staying out of prison.

Some people who are incarcerated say that prison is not that bad and could be worse. They are already paving their way back to the penitentiary before even getting released, because in their minds, they could do another couple of years and still be OK. Their reason is not greater than themselves, so when it comes time to face the challenges life is definitely going to throw their way, they are sure to fail and succumb to the difficulties.

THE WALKING LOGO

Your reason could be that you want to ensure that your parents are able to rely on you in their later years. Your reason could be that you want to make an impact on the lives of people going down the same path you went down. Your reason could be that you want to honor your higher power and be a benefit to the kingdom. Whatever your reason, it has to be something greater than yourself. My main reason to stay out of the penitentiary was to be a father to my son. I did not believe that my son could do another day without having me there and available 24-7.

I did not know the extent to which I would play a role in my son's life, but I knew that I would be relevant. I had not spoken to his mother after the first two years of my ten-year sentence, and I didn't have a clue what level of involvement she would allow. When I contacted her, hearing her voice and the way we conversed on the phone, it was like old times again. This was the greatest challenge because I knew she was in another relationship, and my mind told me that the only reason we weren't together was the prison sentence. I had to check that feeling and focus on being a father to my son and letting her know that I supported her decision to move on and live her life and that I loved her. She was pregnant, so I knew that my time had passed. My time to be a father had not, so that was what I focused on. During my ten years, I had envisioned my life as a free man, enjoying time with my son. That time was here, and I was ready to take on the responsibility of being a father.

Getting established in the lives of your children when you get released will be challenging, but it will be worth it. There can be no transference of information if a positive relationship is not established. The only way you can have influence is through a positive relationship. I knew that I wanted to be the most influential person in my children's lives, rather than the next hot rapper or the people in the neighborhood. Those influences will not get my children in the most desirable place, because they will not give them the right information to make decisions. Those influences will give them the information that will benefit their own agendas. Establishing a positive relationship with your children takes time. You have to allocate the time with them to get to know them, especially since you have been gone.

CARLOS M. CHRISTIAN

Getting established in the courts, if you are not already, is a necessity for any parent coming home from prison. Most people I know had their children out of wedlock, and when that is the case, you have to establish yourself in the courts to protect your rights. When you are married, your rights are already protected. I refer to the term as the "child prenup," which relates to the regular prenuptial agreements that are signed to protect your assets when you marry. If the marriage doesn't survive, you get to keep everything you had before you got married. The child prenup is a term that I made up to say that if the relationship does not survive between the mother of my children and me, then she will not have the ability to take away my rights to be a father.

A child prenup starts with establishing paternity. There are two ways to establish paternity that are recognized by the courts if you had a child out of wedlock. Signing the paternity affidavit that is given to you when the child is born in the hospital along with the birth certificate is one way. The other is taking a DNA test by a recognized agency. The courts will not recognize going on a talk show or purchasing a DNA test out of the store as established paternity.

Once you have established paternity, you can then go to the main court in your city and file for a parenting time order or a shared parenting plan, also known as joint custody in states outside of Ohio. This establishes parenting time with your children regardless of whether you and the mother are together. If she does not honor the parenting time schedule, then she can be held in contempt of court.

Fathers often say that they don't want to get the courts involved in their business, and they are afraid of the courts. This does not put you or your child on a solid foundation. Everything after getting released from prison has to relate to the foundation you are standing on, because shaky ground will cause you to recidivate. Just because things are good with the mother of your children at the time does not guarantee that things will always be good regarding how she feels about you. What if you move on and meet somebody else, and she doesn't want you to be with somebody else? She could say that as long as you are with that person, you cannot see your child. There are mothers who are guided by their feelings and not by their minds. Fathers are arguing and

THE WALKING LOGO

fighting and walking on eggshells to be a part of their children's lives because the mothers are using the children to control them or to get back at them for one reason or another.

Everything was fine with the mother of my son until I had something to say about him not being in town for me to pick him up for school on a Monday. She had gone to her family's house for the weekend, and her car had gotten a flat. She stayed until Monday afternoon, but she was two hours away. I was upset that she didn't let me know on Sunday so that I could've driven there to pick him up and he wouldn't miss school; the way I responded was not good and ended in an argument. She told me not to worry about coming to pick him up at all ever again. She said that she did ten years without me, and she could do another ten.

I didn't take her seriously, and the next day I went to pick him up from school and took him back to my house to do homework and eat dinner like I usually did. I usually took him to his mother's house at around nine thirty. She called me and was still standing on what she had said, and she told me to bring her son to the house right now! I told her that I wouldn't, and the next thing I saw was the police outside the window in the driveway. I answered the door, and they asked me about our son. I told them that I did have him in the house and that I was his father and had the right to parent him. I let the officer know that I was planning to bring our son back to his mother later on that night.

The officer immediately asked for any documentation stating that I had the right to have our son during that time period. I told him that I had signed the birth certificate and other paperwork to establish paternity and paid child support for him. He told me that establishing paternity only gave me the right to pay child support but not the right to parent our child, as we had him out of wedlock. All of those rights are given to the mother in Ohio.

He showed me the Ohio revised code 3109.042, and it stated,

> An unmarried female who gives birth to a child is the sole residential parent and legal custodian of the child until a court of competent jurisdiction issues an order designating another person as the

residential parent and legal custodian. A court designating the residential parent and legal custodian of a child described in this section shall treat the mother and father as standing upon an equality when making the designation.

The only way that I could have a right to parent my son was to go to court and establish myself as the residential parent and legal custodian. After being informed of the law, I told our son to pack his things and go with his mother. I was not about to get arrested and go back to prison, where I would be in a worse situation then I was. The next day I went to the court and filed for custody, and I established myself in the courts with my son soon after. I filed the motion as *pro se*, which means without an attorney, because I didn't have the money to pay an attorney, nor did I have the money to pay any filing fees. I was able to get the filing fees waived through an indigent application because of my low income.

 I went down to the courts with a burning desire to be a father, and because of that, I was able to get a shared parenting plan with our son. I now had fifty-fifty say on what decisions were being made with our child, and my parenting time was allocated through the parenting plan as well. So I would never have the argument again over when I could parent our child.

 After getting the parenting plan established, we never had another discussion about parenting time again. We did not go to trial to get the shared parenting plan established because she ended up coming around. She wasn't comfortable fighting me to be a part of our son's life, and she avoided the trial by agreeing in the mediation. I have had two more children since I have been home, and I automatically set up a shared parenting plan for both of them, even though the relationship was positive with the mother.

 I had to go a few weeks without seeing my son, and I said that I would get established in the lives of my children so I would not go through that again, although our relationship rebounded after a few weeks, and we were able to get it done through mediation. I vowed not to wait until that could possibly happen again and got it done when the relationship was in a good place, so there would be no time missed between my children and me. One parent is not greater than the other, and both parents are instrumental to the development of that child. I could not place the blame on anybody but me if I was not involved in my children's lives. When something matters, you will find out what you need in order to get it done. The only way that I wasn't going to be a part of my children's lives was if there was no more breath in my body.

The next important area in establishing yourself with your children is communicating with your child-support enforcement agency (CSEA). This has to be as serious as communicating with your probation officer. If your order is calculated too high, communicating with the CSEA will be the best thing to do in order to request a modification. When you don't communicate with them, then actions will be taken against you that can throw you off track in establishing the relationship with your children.

Fathers have told me that they believe that because they are behind in their child support, they cannot see their children. Nothing could be further from the truth. Child support and parenting time are two separate entities. Being behind on child support does not void your right to parent your child during the scheduled time that has been allotted through the courts.

When I was released, I didn't know the importance of communicating with child support, and I figured that because they were taking money from me when I was incarcerated, they would do the same thing when I was released. I thought they would just automatically take the money from my checks from my job. I didn't know that I had to go to the agency and provide the information about my employment and where I was living. I didn't do any of those things, and they sent written communication to my last known address, which was the halfway house in Cleveland. They considered that notifying me. Needless to say, I never got the communication, and child support went about their disciplinary actions against me.

I figured out that I had a problem when I was driving one day, and the police pulled me over and told me the license plates that were registered in my name indicated my license had been suspended by the department of child support services. The officer allowed me to drive home and advised me to take care of the situation. I then immediately contacted child support and let them know that I didn't know about me missing payments and that I thought they would take it out of my check. They advised me that it didn't work like that, and I had to pay three months of child support payments to get my license back. I did what they required.

Shortly after that, they made a mistake and cleared all of my money out of my checking account. It did not register that I had made the three-month payment, and they were treating me as if I were still delinquent. They sent the money to my son's mother. She never pressed child support, but she had to give my name when she was on assistance when I was incarcerated, so I had to make the minimum payment of fifty dollars. If I had communicated with CSEA when I first came home, I would have been able to avoid the drama I did not need in my life. Not knowing is not an excuse. It is your responsibility to know, because when the hammer comes down, it isn't going to spare you because you don't know.

I felt like I was doing a great job with my son. I came home and bought all his school clothes, and I took him to school every day. I got his sports equipment for football. I wasn't thinking about child support; I figured that his mom wasn't thinking about it either because of the work I was doing with our son. It came out that she wasn't thinking about it, and I wasn't thinking about it, but the department was thinking about me.

One thing about being a father and embracing this great responsibility is that it kept me focused on staying home and valuing my freedom in spite of all of the challenges. I was able to see my children grow, and nothing has been quite as fulfilling for me as a man. Children don't ask for all the money in the world. They don't want you to be the toughest gangster. They just honestly want you to be their dad, and having them involved helps you overcome the odds of recidivating. The people you have around you once you get released must support your mission in becoming the person who contradicts prison.

6

For Better or for Worse

PEOPLE OFTEN UNDERESTIMATE how much attention must be paid to picking the right partner to move forward with in life. If you get released from prison as a single person, as so many people do, it is best to know what you are looking for in a partner. Knowing what that other person requires in a partner is important as well. You do not want to spend your most valuable asset—time—attempting to build a relationship when the two of you want different things out of life and are going in different directions. The time spent trying to convince the other that your direction is best would be better spent going in that direction with somebody who is in agreement. Not everybody is going in the same direction, and what is good for you may not be good for the other person.

We get into a bad space when we attempt to control somebody else. That never leads to success, just more stress. The greatest challenge is controlling yourself, and that will take all your energy and attention. Focusing on controlling someone else takes away from the amount of time needed to control yourself, leaving you out of control. Successful people control themselves. They put in countless hours honing their craft when they have the urge to do something else that could be more pleasing. They control who they allow into their environments, where they place themselves, which problems they are going to address, how they go about their everyday business, and ultimately how their time is spent. They never make the excuse that somebody else made them do anything. It was them; they made the choice. The bottom line is that successful people control themselves. They do not leave control in the hands of other people or systems, because they understand that they will not get the best deal when they allow that to happen.

Nobody has the room to be out of control—especially when you are making the transition into society as a returning citizen. Relationships that are not productive can leave you in a terrible place where you are not even valuing freedom anymore. The constant fighting and tension in the environment between you and your significant other can be draining, causing you to recidivate. People will be who they are going to be, and if they show you who they are, then it is wise to believe them and make your decisions regarding the continuance of the relationship based on that information. The reason so many returning citizens fail in making the transition to society is because of the people they choose as their significant others. If my significant other does not respect me because I am making minimum wage, then I might attempt to do something illegal to earn more money to get her respect.

In the movie *Dead Presidents*, actor Larenz Tate's character was pressured by the mother of his children to earn more money than he was earning at the butcher shop where he worked. He had just come back from the Vietnam War, and he was trying to get readjusted to society. His girlfriend had a boyfriend while he was gone, but she gave Larenz Tate's character her time instead. The pressure of not feeling secure in his position as a man because of his girlfriend's down talk led Larenz Tate's character to orchestrate the heist of a Brinks truck. He was later caught and received life in prison. There's a good chance the girlfriend went on to find another man, and his end result was prison.

It would have made all the difference in the world if she had applauded him for going to work, putting forth that effort to support his family, and making the decision to come home every night. Nothing happens overnight, and both you and your significant other must understand that getting to the extravagant event you envisioned in your future is a process. Patience is the key for both parties.

THE WALKING LOGO

I have seen people whose significant others promoted them to go back to the streets to make money rather than committing to the process. You must be meticulous when it comes to choosing whom you are going to make your significant other. It can make the difference between progression and regression. We don't want to focus on changing people but rather enhancing them, and your significant other should offer the same.

I got involved with a woman when I first came home. She was from the rough neighborhoods in Cleveland, Ohio, and her mind was stuck there. When she came over to the house, she would look out the window like she was on the run. She was smoking marijuana like a hippie back in the seventies. Her looks were great, but where she was mentally was not going to make our relationship successful. She was not into a family at the time; all she wanted to do was have fun. I could not be upset with her for being where she was, but it wasn't where I was trying to be, so I chose to stop contacting her. I told myself I didn't have the time to be in a relationship like that, because if I spent too much time with her, I would begin to do what she was doing. I could not afford to do that with where I was coming from.

She didn't have any true ambition to get better in life, and at the time, she was content where she was, which was struggling. I also didn't want to get back in the habit of smoking marijuana, as that would throw me off my path to success. That was an expense I could not afford if I wanted to be successful. If I was around my lady, who smoked constantly, the power of influence would be too strong, and more than likely, I would succumb to the temptation. The interaction with her was brief, and I moved on rather quickly once I understood. She was beautiful and young, with no children, but it was not a fit for me because of where she was in her life and where I was in mine. I was twenty-nine years old and building my life with a ten-year-old son who needed my attention. I had different responsibilities than she did. It didn't make her less; it just made her not for me.

Your partner will be around you for the majority of your time, so you must choose this individual with care. If you do not put any thought into this decision, then there will likely be issues that could have been avoided if you two had had a discussion. Understanding what that other person is willing to do in a relationship is vital; it saves time spent in toxic relationships.

Writing a list of what I expected from the person I wanted to build a future with is an idea that was introduced to me later in my journey, after I had gone through a divorce. It made all the sense in the world, and when I look back on my relationship with my ex-wife, the time we spent arguing could have been avoided if we had made out the lists to see what each of us expected of the other.

This is being responsible with your time and your decisions. It's huge when you understand what you must have in a partner to make it work before you go surveying the market, as you've already gone through the vigorous process of understanding yourself. This takes research and being around others who have successful relationships. Understanding others helps you further understand yourself. You will see some things in other people's relationships that you won't want in your own relationship.

I met my now ex-wife in August when I came home, and we moved in together by October. We spent roughly two months getting to know each other before making such a big decision. I went through the list in my mind, and she passed it, so I made the decision to build a life with her. My list was not extensive, nor was it well thought out. I was satisfied with her having a job, a house, one child, and a pretty face. I should have inquired about the roles we would play in the lives of our children (whom we had by different people), which was vital to the success of our relationship. We had a child together, and we spent the next eight years in intense arguments. We went to the Bahamas on family cruises, and we argued even on vacation.

She assumed that my son would just come over on the weekends until I arranged with his mother to get him full-time. This was an issue we didn't address when we were making the decision to move in together, because I assumed that if I got the opportunity to get my son more, she would welcome the idea. She was not against the idea as much as she was against it happening that soon. I would not have moved in if I had known that it would not be OK for my son to be there full-time.

THE WALKING LOGO

She would not have pushed for me to move in if she had known that I wanted to capitalize on the opportunity to have my son there full time. Her son had just seen his dad leave a few months earlier, and then he would have to see another family come in and claim space in the house. In retrospect I could see how she was concerned about how that could negatively affect him. I was concerned that if I had the opportunity to get my son and didn't, and he saw me with her son 24-7, that would negatively affect his development. We both had legitimate reasons to stand on, and if we'd had this discussion beforehand, we would have avoided a lot of heartache. Rushing into any decision is not good, especially when you are making a decision that will directly affect the lives of others.

The focus should be on getting to know what you want in your significant other before making that commitment. Your primary commitment coming home should be to establish a positive relationship with the mother of your children to effectively coparent or, if you do not have children, to establish that relationship with yourself in order to get stable. You do not want to go and get involved with somebody and then be in need of a crutch because you did not establish your foundation, because that will usually put a strain on the relationship.

When I moved in with my now ex-wife, I made it clear that I was going to get my name on the lease and on the utilities that I was paying. I have seen so many guys sleeping in their cars because they were kicked out of the house. Usually it is because while they pay bills and contribute, they do not have their names on anything in the house, so when the women get upset, they kick them out, only to tell them to come back in a couple of days. I always said, "If you kick me out, it will take a redoing of the lease because it is my right to be there as well. Not only that, but if I go, the electric, gas, water, cable, and phone goes with me." I was bluffing, but I was taken seriously. We had our disagreements, but I would sleep on the couch rather than sleep in the streets. You should always stand on solid ground so that people cannot rock you.

It is OK to tell the people who are interested in building a life with you that you need some time to get acclimated with society and to establish yourself. If they are truly for you, they will be there when the time is right. You don't want to come home and be the everything for anybody because you aren't in a position for that. Relationships are a responsibility and should not be taken lightly. You have to be mentally ready to take on a serious, monogamous relationship, and that all begins with knowing exactly what you are willing to do and what you expect from another person.

7

Financial Freedom

THE CONCEPT OF money was mentioned 140 times in the Bible. Money is important. One of the main reasons people get incarcerated is due to their relationship with money. Money is not the root of all evil—the love of money is. Any way you slice the pie, money will be relevant, and it will be relevant once you get released from prison and make the transition.

Financial freedom can improve the quality of your life. The problem is not money. The problem is the way we view money. Money is a tool that helps enrich your life, so not being financially stable can cause some stress. I used to think that money was all that I needed to solve my problems until I realized that the way we think actually solves our problems. Money is important, but so are your health and positive relationships. You must put money in its proper place to be able to overcome the challenges of transitioning back into society. You must understand that it has its place and properly manage it.

People say that money doesn't matter. I would like to hear them say that when the gas bill is due or they go to the gas station or the grocery store. I'm pretty sure that once they get to any of these places, they will soon understand that money does matter.

When you don't respect money, it doesn't respect you, and you will be without it, and your life won't click as you desire it to. In raising my children, I let them know about the importance of money and what it is used for. I implemented a program in my household a few years back with my children, named "The Double Up," to get them to understand the importance of saving and investing. I gave them allowance every week, and I encouraged them to either save it or find something to invest in to make more money. At any undisclosed time, I would approach them and say, "Double up." Whatever they had saved, I would double it up. If they had twenty dollars saved, I would give them another twenty so they would have forty dollars. If they had fifty dollars saved, I would give them another fifty, and so on and so on. I was getting them to understand the importance of taking care of their money and stretching and maximizing every dollar they had.

When I approached them with the opportunity to double up, either they were ready to capitalize on the opportunity or they were content with where they spent their money. I developed the program to encourage proper management of money. They saw how they could capitalize on the opportunity to get more money because they were saving, and that improved their decision-making process concerning money.

Misunderstanding the purpose of money and how to use this powerful tool can have your life in chaos and make you unsure of yourself. Some people use money to get people to validate them. Money cannot truly validate you. Some people depend on money to build positive relationships. Money alone cannot accomplish that. Money is not everything, but it is important, and it demands your attention in your journey to become successful. Before I was incarcerated, I thought money was everything, and so I sacrificed relationships and my health to obtain it. That was where the error in my thinking lay, so that is where the destruction occurred—from the value I placed on money.

The difference between me and other people who were selling drugs when I was a teenager was my ability to "stack," a term used on the streets that means "to save money." I looked to minimize unnecessary costs and cut out the middlemen. I understood that the middlemen were costly, and I avoided them any time I could. Those who get hustled on the streets do not make it very long, and I was always aware of the money that was coming in and how it went out. You could not sell me anything at any price, because I knew the prices of the products. Having that knowledge put me in a position to come out on top in my dealings.

THE WALKING LOGO

People make a killing off those who don't know and are green to the game. They overcharge those who are ignorant of the prices and willing to pay them. This type of character in the streets is considered a sucker, and they are continuously treated as such, with a lack of respect.

Getting released and viewing the way that money works in general society, I quickly found that it is similar to the way it works in the underworld. What you do not know will put you in an undesirable position, which is usually watching your money in someone else's pocket when it should be in yours. You cannot go on that vacation, because you unnecessarily gave other people too much money. You cannot get that new car, because you unnecessarily gave other people too much money. The people you gave that money to will get that new car and go on that vacation, and they genuinely don't care what you or your family can't do, as long as they can do what they desire with your money.

Paying attention to what businesses attempt to convince you to believe is small is the first step to becoming financially stable. They will say, "It's just a small fee to pay." I would challenge that if it's small for me, then it should be small and insignificant to them as well, and letting me keep it in my own pocket is OK. That won't happen, because the wealthy understand the value of the penny, and the poor disrespect the penny and see it as insignificant. It is a mind-set with money. If you don't properly handle that which is small, then you likely won't properly handle that which is big. If you waste a penny, you will likely waste a dollar as well. It is a way of thinking.

Some wise words stuck with me, although I cannot remember the source. It is best to attack a problem when it is small and doesn't take that much to overcome rather than attempt to attack that same problem when it has become so big that it overwhelms you. You cannot get big without being small. With money, it is necessary that we value the small in order to get the big. With that mind-set, I avoided fees and interest everywhere it was possible and made the best sense. I transferred my basic street knowledge over to regular society once I came home, and it put me in a desirable place. I could recognize the shady legal hustles, and I stayed away from them because of the knowledge that I sought out and obtained.

The first thing that everybody who gets released from prison should do is get a checking account. It is estimated that nine million Americans do not have a checking account. Coming from prison, you don't want to be one of those nine million, especially when you are trying to get established. The last thing you need is to pay someone to cash your check or spend your money, which is the case with prepaid cards. You have to pay fees to make purchases, withdrawals, and card replacement fees, to name just a few.

Opening a checking or savings account at a bank helps you avoid paying those fees. Although you'll hear that it's just a small fee of three dollars to cash your check, it's too much when you can cash it for no charge at your bank. Those small fees add up, just like small problems turn into big problems. Protect your small money so you can have the mind-set to protect your big money.

When you establish an account, be sure that the bank is easily accessible in your area. This is to ensure that when you go to the ATM to withdraw cash from your account, you don't get charged fees because you are at a different bank's machine. When you withdraw cash from a foreign ATM, which simply means that you bank at Chase and withdraw cash from a Huntington ATM, you get charged a fee from Huntington and one from your bank as well.

I got released in Cleveland, Ohio, and established a checking account at Charter One, which was easily accessible in Cleveland. When I moved to Columbus, Ohio, it seemed like the only one in the entire city was all the way across town from where I was living. When I needed to make withdrawals, I had to go to another bank's ATM for convenience rather than spending the gas to drive all the way across town. The issue of spending that convenience fee lasted for about two transactions before I closed the account and transferred to a Chase checking account that was everywhere across the city.

You don't want to pay fees for having the actual account, either. Sometimes banks charge fees for account maintenance. When I was looking for free checking, I meant free checking, and I wouldn't take anything less. I was aware of the slick talk because I dealt with grown men with habits when I was thirteen years old. There was no ambiguous language, because I made it clear with the banker and I asked whether there was any way that the account would charge me for having it. When they said no and explained it in writing, I was comfortable banking with the bank.

Having a checking account is the first step to getting away from the brown-paper-bag-stashed-under-your-mattress type of life that doesn't put you in the most desirable place. Somebody can steal your cash, but if somebody robs the bank, your money is insured by the FDIC, so you will not lose anything.

After getting your checking account established, you want to look at different strategies to save money for the purpose of investment. I practiced a program that I implemented when I first came home, where I would increase the amount that I was saving by a dollar every week and put it in my savings. This is something I started at the beginning of the year. In the first week, you put a dollar away. The second week, you put two dollars away. The third week, you put three dollars away. Whatever the week of the year it is, that's how much money goes into your savings, all the way up to week fifty-two. If you do that then, you will have saved a total of $1,378 in the year. I then took my savings and made investments in different investment vehicles.

I went to a banker who told me to get a certificate of deposit (CD), which is a time deposit, a financial product commonly sold in the United States and elsewhere by banks, thrift institutions, and credit unions. It has a maturity date of your choosing, and I chose a six-month maturity date. When I looked at the amount I made in interest, I was disappointed to see it was only a few dollars. I felt like it was the same as burying the money in the ground because of how little interest the CD earned.

That same banker then told me to invest in a mutual fund because of my age. It would give me exposure to the stock market. A mutual fund is a professionally managed investment fund that pools money from many investors to purchase securities. So instead of me picking the stocks to buy and trade, the team managing the mutual fund chooses what stocks to invest my money in to make a profit. When I researched the team managing the fund, I saw that they were performing well compared to some of the others, so I chose them.

I met another financial adviser, and he told me that I could cut out the middleman and create my own portfolio. I could get a Scottrade account and buy my own shares in the different companies. Scottrade is a privately owned American discount brokerage firm that operates both online and at retail locations. I want to make a disclaimer that I am not a financial adviser, and I would suggest you seek professional advisers before making investments to truly understand how these investment instruments operate.

I was buying my own shares in different companies that I saw and knew were doing well. I invested in Walmart, Conagra Foods, and United Airlines (before they merged with Continental Airlines to form the largest airline in the country). I was excited about buying the shares low, and when they rose up about a dollar, I would sell. It was sort of a rush for me.

At one point, I was making about $400 on each trade. Once I sold them and the price dropped back down, I would buy the same shares and repeat the process. Then I was introduced to what is known as penny stocks, and I made about $1,800 on one trade. I took everything out of my staple stocks, which are less volatile, and invested everything in the penny stocks. I was determined to get rich in ten days, not ten years.

This was against the advice of the financial adviser I met at the bank, who made me aware of the ability to trade my stocks in the first place. He gave me a couple of rules to never forsake. He said that investment money is investment money, and bill money is bill money. Never integrate your money. He also said that diversity is the key when it comes to your portfolio. Never go completely high risk, and do not stay completely low risk.

I stayed true to not integrating my money and left my bill money alone, but I took all of my investment money and put it all in the penny stock that I had made the $1,800 from the previous day. The bottom fell out, and I lost about $12,000 dollars of my investment. My heart was in my stomach, but it was a lesson learned. It was an expensive lesson, but it was still a lesson. Investing is good when you know what you're doing. I would encourage people getting released from prison to do research on how to invest so that your money can actually work for you.

One of the most important areas of your finances to help you keep more of your money in your pocket is establishing your credit. There are three types of credit that will impact your credit score, which ranges from 300 to 850.

THE WALKING LOGO

These are revolving accounts, which are primarily credit cards; installment loans, which are primarily car payments or personal loans; and mortgages, which are home loans. You will need a mixture of all three to eventually have A1 credit. Your credit score will determine whether you will pay $17,220 for a $10,000 automobile loan over a five-year period with a 25 percent annual percentage rate (APR) or a total of $10,740 for the same car with a 3 percent APR over the course of five years.

    The difference is that you will be able to drive your car to make money, and it is reliable transportation. You didn't have the $10,000 to buy a car outright, but with the good credit, you can finance the vehicle for a total of $740. You are getting charged $740 to hold $10,000 for five years. The person with the bad credit who has to pay 25 percent APR is getting charged $7,220 to hold the $10,000 for five years. It's the same $10,000 dollars, but one is paying more than the other based on the credit score. That is why buying that 1995 Buick Regal for $1,750 when I first came home was the best move, because I didn't have any established credit, and that is in the same category as bad credit when applying for a loan. There was no way I could get on my feet if I was paying $7,220 in interest. Some people focus on the manageable monthly payment rather than your APR for the loan. Your APR is the most important information that you will need before you sign any paperwork.

    The first step in establishing your credit is pulling your credit report. Everybody can get one free credit report per year through annualcreditreport.com. Your credit report will inform you of what accounts are on your credit. When you look at your credit report, look at the addresses and other key identifiers. If you see an address that is not yours, then there is a good chance that somebody has used your name to open a credit account. It is important that you challenge these fraudulent accounts and remove them from your credit report by filing a dispute with the credit bureaus.

    There are three major credit bureaus that creditors report to: Experian, Equifax, and TransUnion. Make sure that the information is accurate on all three credit reports from the three different credit bureaus.

    The next step is putting good credit on your report. I made sure that I got an unsecured credit card to begin to establish good credit. It had a lot of fees because of my lack of credit, and it was for beginners, so the APR was high (38 percent interest for purchases). I got the card anyway because I needed to get started. It was the same concept as employment, meaning you might not get the high-salary job in the beginning, but you must get started nonetheless.

Slow motion at a minimum-wage job beats no motion waiting for the right job. Establishing credit takes time, and you want to get started immediately. Although I could not get out of the membership fees, maintenance fees, and processing fees that the card charged, I read the fine print that stated that if I paid my entire statement balance each billing cycle each month, then I would not have to pay the 38 percent interest for my purchases. That meant my purchases were dollar for dollar.

On your statement, it gives you a choice to either pay your statement balance or the minimum payment. I wondered what the difference was. The difference is that whether you will get charged interest or no interest for your purchases. When you pay the statement balance in full, you get charged no interest. When you pay the minimum payment, you get charged the 38 percent interest. If I made $100 in purchases during that billing cycle, and I paid the $100 off when my bill was due, I did not get charged any interest. If I made the $100 in purchases and paid the $10 minimum payment, then I would get charged $38 in interest. So although my account would be in good standing because I made the required payments, my pockets would not be in good standing because my money was in the pockets of the credit-card company versus my own.

It was like a light bulb went off when I understood this concept, and I wondered why people were afraid of credit cards. It was not the credit cards that were the problem but the people using them. The excellent payment history that I displayed with the beginner credit card got the interest of better credit-card companies that did not have any fees. I used the same concept of paying my statement balance each month to avoid interest.

Making payments on time is important in establishing your credit, but I made it just as important to pay the statement balance to avoid the interest as well. I was able to pay the statement balance each month because I spent only on my credit cards and not out of my checking account. My checks from my employer were direct deposited into my checking account each week, and I didn't touch them. I made all my purchases on my credit cards, so when the time came to pay the statement balance, I had a surplus in my checking account. I just transferred the money from my checking account to my credit card each month. I was disciplined to not spend in two places, which would be spending from my checking account and spending on my credit cards. I told myself something different from what the credit-card companies told me, which was that they provided the opportunity for extra spending power. I viewed the available credit as my money and not extra money. I still spent within my budget. Thinking of credit card money as extra spending money is a sure way to not have the money to pay the statement balance and be forced to pay the minimum payment and get charged the interest.

I closed the beginner's credit card account. It got me in the door with the better credit-card companies, so it served its purpose. I paid my dues, and it was time to move on in my journey to obtaining excellent credit.

Once my credit behavior on my credit cards elevated my credit score to 728, which was considered very good back in 2009, I was able to open the second part of my credit mix, which was securing an installment loan for an automobile. I received a 5 percent interest rate on the car, and I didn't have to put any money down, nor did I have to trade my other car in. I felt confident when I was negotiating, because they were trying to get my Buick Regal as a trade-in, but my good credit gave me leverage, and I kept the Buick and drove off the lot with the new car as well. I ended up selling the Regal for $600 privately, but it was better than giving it to the car lot to sell and getting nothing from the sale.

People are sometimes so happy to get a new car that they don't care about their old cars. They trade them in with no problem because they feel that they're not worth much, and they are focused on the newer cars. They end up giving the older car away to the dealer when they could have put it up for sale on the Internet and gotten more for it. "Every penny counts" is the mind-set I adopted when I was in the streets, where others looked down on the customers who had a handful of change. I accepted it with no hesitation. I transferred that same attitude to the general society, and it has been beneficial.

Shortly after I got my installment loan, I purchased a home with my fiancée. The home loan was the last of the lines of credit that boosted my credit score to 768 about six months into it. It initially plummeted, but then it rebounded to a level that it had never been at before. I had the mind-set that if I were going to be paying for where I stayed, I would rather pay to own than rent it. When I left the rental property, I would be lucky to get the security deposit. Home ownership is a good move to make when you are establishing yourself financially. Even if I chose to leave, I would be able to either rent the property out or sell it and potentially recoup the money that I invested. You do not have that option with a rental property. Plus the houses that are for rent are often not paid off. When you pay your rent to somebody, you are paying their mortgage. The rent is always going to be higher than the mortgage payment.

It takes a two-year work history to secure a home loan. I would suggest that you do your time paying rent, but be focused on purchasing your own house. The beauty in purchasing your own home is that your options increase for where you will live. When I was renting, landlords denied me because of my felony record. The landlords who accepted my application were in the rougher neighborhoods.

Establishing yourself financially will be a necessity once you get released, and it will make a great difference in the quality of your life. The best way to do that is to keep the attitude of avoiding fees by any means necessary, keeping interest as low as possible, and paying attention to the pennies because they add up to dollars.

8

The Speed of Recovery

Falling isn't what really makes you fail; it's not getting back up when you do. It's not about running a race and finding yourself off the track that matters the most. It's not realizing or not making the decision to get back on track to continue the race. If you don't continue, then it's impossible to be a victor. The journey to successfully transition back into society is challenging, and it throws all different kinds of pitches at you to swing at, and sometimes you'll strike out. What you do after that will make all the difference in the world. Either you adjust so you can hit the pitch the next time because you've learned what you have done wrong, or you swing the same way when you get back up to the plate and get the same result. Before you know it, the game will be over, and you will lose.

The speed of your recovery will determine whether you succeed or fail and get reincarcerated. The longer it takes you to recover from a mistake, the greater the chance that you will find yourself in despair and not even attempt to recover but continue on the path of recidivism. The challenge is to do right when everyone around you is doing wrong or to tell the truth when everyone is telling lies.

The majority of people get released with the mind-set that they will do the right thing to avoid another prison term, but so many fail to stick to the plan and eventually get reincarcerated. It's like when babies come into the world. The more babies grow and mature, the more they take on the ways of the world and their environment. Babies who try to walk are not concerned with what people think about them falling in their attempts. They are not afraid to get up and try again because they are in their own world, and it is all about what they are attempting to accomplish. When they are attempting to talk, they don't care about fumbling the words or how foolish it can sound to an experienced orator. They are focused on getting the task accomplished independent of how people perceive them. As they experience more time in the world, they start to care about how people perceive them, and it affects their willingness to try things.

I believe that is why it is said that children are closest to God; because of their ability to do whatever they deem necessary, to them anything is possible. We have been created in God's image, and I truly believe this is how we are supposed to go at life. Our environment influences us to not try this or that, and we are handicapped by our fear of failure and confined by what people say is logical.

You can come home and be positive, but when you have more negative interactions with people and situations, it can lead to you being tempted to just fall in line with the way that things are in your environment. You might come home and be really set on working a traditional job, and you get the job, and then you get fired. How do you respond? The opportunity was difficult to obtain in the first place, and you put your best effort forward to retain the employment. These types of challenges can cause you to maybe relapse into your old behavior and handle your situation according to how you used to handle situations.

I have mentored people who were addicted to drugs before their incarceration and who had remained sober when they were incarcerated but had been unable to overcome the challenges and temptations of the world upon their release. They had relapsed and began to use again. After that they had to make important decisions about how to remain free and not end up back in prison. They recognized what they were doing and that it would not lead to where they wanted to be in life, so they adjusted.

Adjustment is analyzing what triggered the error and then avoiding that trigger in the future. Their speed of recovery was fast, and they did not sit on

THE WALKING LOGO

their errors before they addressed them and changed. Their mind-set was that even though they failed, it was not over for them, and they were not failures. Failure is not a person but an event. If those people told themselves that they were failures, then they would no longer be interested in succeeding, and they would continue to get high.

People with the latter mind-set in the same situation often find their speed of recovery to be too slow. Life overwhelms them so much that they end up returning back to prison. They feel as if, because they made errors and did what they said they wouldn't do, they no longer have a reason to try to do what they believe is right. They don't know that if they survive the errors and still have breath in their bodies, then they still have time to right their wrongs. You have to understand that it is possible, and it is necessary. Just as there are no perfect human beings on the face of the earth, it is not wise to think that you will not make an error on your journey to becoming a restored citizen. You want to limit your errors and truly work to run the perfect race, but if you happen to get displaced off the track, you must get back on and continue to run your race.

Understanding that you are off track and what the consequences are for that is mandatory to your speed of recovery. That is why it's important to be connected to people who are running in the right direction, one that matches your desires to end up where you want to be in life. If you are running in the wrong direction, then they will let you know because you won't see them in front of you or to your sides. They don't have to say a word. The way they are running their race says it all. Stopping and turning around to run in the opposite direction is taking the time to analyze yourself and fix the error. Without being connected to the right people, it is likely that you will continue to run in the same direction without believing that it will lead you miles and miles off your destination.

When I found myself partying when I first came home and hung with the people who were going in the opposite direction of where I wanted to be in life, I temporarily ran in that direction as well. I was in the clubs and drinking, and I enjoyed the chants of my old friends and how they were receiving me, and I began to act like I used to preincarceration. This is the character that they knew, and this was the character I believed they were calling for. I would get to the door at the club, and there would be a cover charge. I would let them know that I would not pay because of who I was. After all, I was Frank Nitti, and I went at things a certain way. If the drinks weren't coming fast enough, I went behind the bar and would be about to pour my own drink before the bartender rushed over and waited on me. This behavior was cheered on by those old friends in the same old places.

If I hadn't had people in place to tell me that I was out of control, I could've continued down that path of destruction. I analyzed myself, and I told myself that I was a father who had just completed a ten-year prison sentence, and neither my son nor I could afford for me to spend another day in prison.

Sometimes you slip, but it is your responsibility to recognize the slip and not stumble on the same stumbling block in your future. People will laugh and say that you have not changed and that you are still the same person that you used to be because you have done some of the same things, but you must be encouraged by the work that you have put in on yourself. The foundation of the work that you put in is in simply establishing an actual track that will get you to your desired location. Before when you did those things, you didn't even have a track established in your mind, so there was no getting back on track.

Now when you do those things, you have a track established in your mind that will convince you and urge you to get back on it to get to your desired location. As you grow stronger in your journey, you won't even make those same old errors. You will make new errors. The speed of your recovery after your fall will make all the difference in the world to your success.

9

The Greatest Responsibility

You're on a plane with your one-year-old child in the passenger seat next to you, and the plane begins to go down. The plane has only one oxygen mask that works, and the person who gets it will survive, but the person who doesn't could possibly die from a shortage of breath because of the cabin losing pressure. Who do you put the oxygen mask on first, you or your child?

I ask this question all the time in the parenting class I teach about how to establish a positive relationship with their children. Most of the time, the immediate answer is put it on the child, of course. Parents feel like they have lived their lives, and it is meant for their children to live their lives now. They said that they would take the chance of losing their breath versus taking the chance of their children losing theirs. It sounds heroic and admirable, but it doesn't make any sense.

If you have ever been on a plane, when they give the instructions on what to do in case of a crisis, they clearly state to secure yourself first before any children. If you are not secure, then how can you ensure that your children will be secure? It would be best to take a breath from the oxygen mask, and then put it on your child once you have gotten the air needed to stay conscious. The reason this makes the most sense is that if you put the mask on your one-year-old first, and then you pass out, who will ensure that your child will keep the mask on? The other passengers will be busy taking care of themselves and their families. That will leave your child alone, not understanding the importance of having the oxygen mask on and possibly ending up unconscious because nobody is there to assist. That means that your child's best chance of survival is having you there!

Taking care of yourself is the best chance you will have to take care of your child or anybody else whom you love. We are often conditioned to believe that it is selfish to include yourself on the list of people whom you should be taking care of in your life. If you allow yourself to be run into the ground, then the people you want to help and support won't have you around to do so.

When you get released from the penitentiary, there is often a certain level of guilt that causes people to overextend themselves in attempts to make up for not being there. They take on bills they don't have the ability to pay because they are not completely solidified yet to do so. People will pile their problems on you as if they wouldn't be able to solve them if you weren't there, even though they figured out a way when you were incarcerated. Everybody will be happy for you to be home and will have something for you to do to benefit them. You have to be careful and not feel obligated to the point that you drown yourself in other people's demands and needs.

People will have the best chance to get the best help from you if you are properly taken care of and have the ability to exhibit the best expression of yourself. The greatest responsibility that you will have above all else once you get released from prison is to take care of yourself first. I'm not saying not to help anyone. I'm saying that in order to truly help someone, you must help yourself first, so that you can be effective in your assistance. If it fits into your schedule and you are able to do it, by all means do it, but the challenge is when you do not have time in your schedule or the resources to do it, and you still do it because of the guilt trip that was placed on you.

This type of experience can rob you from having the appreciation of your opportunity to be free, and you could find yourself going back to doing what you did before your incarceration. I have seen fathers and mothers get released from prison and go back to selling drugs or robbing people because they could not make ends meet with their current jobs; they couldn't cope with the demands to immediately fill their roles in the house as far as paying bills. I

THE WALKING LOGO

had a famous saying, "It ain't them times," when I was asked to do something that I knew would put a stretch on me and compromise my sanity. You will hear some grumbling and face disagreement from your loved ones and even your children, but you must be disciplined enough to know the importance of establishing a positive relationship with yourself and get it done.

The first thing that you must do to take care of yourself is to figure out what you like to do that puts your mind at ease. It can be something as simple as sitting in the driveway at night with the music playing in your car. It could be reading books by your favorite author. It could be cooking and eating a nice meal of your choice. I know some people who said fishing relaxed them and put their minds at ease. It could be going camping or even going on vacations to an island. I make sure that I watch the Cleveland Browns every Sunday despite them losing and people asking me why I waste my time watching them lose every week.

What I like to do may not be something that you like to do or think is important, but that's why it's necessary to figure out what matters to you and what puts you at ease. If you leave it up to other people, they will base their advice about what you should do to take care of yourself on their own preferences, leaving you grumpy and not feeling like you are living an enriched life.

Once you figure out what you like to do that will put your mind at ease, then you must implement time into your schedule and stick to it! You are responsible for your own schedule, so along with working and taking care of your responsibilities, you must do the things that take care of you. The greatest responsibility that you will encounter as an adult is taking care of you.

As a single dad, I find it challenging to make time to take care of myself while having my eight-year-old son throughout the week, taking him to his mother on the weekends, and taking care of my two-year-old daughter in the evening time when her mother goes to work, but I make sure I get it done. It helps with how I view life and the experience that people have when they interact with me. I take my son to summer camp in the morning, and then he plays football in the evening. When I pick him up from summer camp, he has about an hour before I take him to football practice, and he will ask me to take him swimming in between. He doesn't mean any harm. He is just focused on getting done what he wants to get done. It is my responsibility to say no so that I have some time to relax before I take him to practice and cook dinner. I am responsible for knowing whether I have taken care of myself, because no one will care as much as I do.

I make sure that my regimen will put me in the best headspace to be productive in my life. As soon as I wake up in the morning, I listen to a powerful message, usually on YouTube, from a motivational speaker. After that, I usually read a few pages of a book that will help exercise my mind and increase my vocabulary, and finally I go to exercise at the gym. All this helps me be in a place of productivity. Your mind is the greatest tool you have, because it will dictate where you will be in life. It is best that you invest in it.

You must protect your mind by protecting your environment. When I was in prison, I had to be around people who were antagonistic because of how they felt about me or a football team that I liked. When the Cleveland Browns came on television, they always cheered for the other team with the intention of making me upset. They were pushing to see my team lose versus pushing to see their team win. Their team could be playing on another channel, but they would rather watch the Browns lose than watch their team win. It taught me that people will allow hate to drive them rather than love because of how they feel about themselves.

You can make your reality whatever you choose. You have been given the mind to be able to get that done. Some people are negative because they feel like they have to settle in life, and they want others to feel negative about life as well. Some people are just negative, and when you do an inventory of the people in your life, you have to make sure they are not occupying prime space in your environment. They will be draining and turn your experience on this earth unpleasant. It is your responsibility to remove them from your environment. As long as they are the way they are, it will always make you uncomfortable, and you must have the discipline to move on.

If you know a conversation is going in a direction that is not beneficial to how you view yourself, you have to shut it down. I have deleted text messages before reading them because I knew they would be negative, because the person was upset when he or she sent them. Feelings change, and people come

THE WALKING LOGO

back once they do and say they didn't mean what they said, but the scars are still there. I protect my mind by not reading that mess, because if I do, it can put me in a bad space. If I leave it in my phone, I might be tempted to read it, so I automatically delete it to protect myself from myself.

When you have all the things that are working against you coming from prison, you cannot afford to work against yourself. If you are not working against yourself, then you can overcome anything, and this is the key. I fight the enemy within on a continuous basis to render the enemy outside myself harmless. You must know the contribution that you desire to make in this world and to your family, and if you don't take care of yourself, you will not accomplish it. The most valuable time that you have is not yesterday, nor is it tomorrow. It is right now! Take advantage of right now by using the experiences from your past to make better decisions in your "right now," and use the future as motivation to keep fighting and striving in the "right now."

If you are in a situation that you feel is bad, then you must intentionally do something to make it better. If you do not like the bad, then you will not like the worse, and if you do not maximize your "right now," it will be worse. Overcoming prison or any other challenging situation depends solely on your making up your mind to do so. Be sure you are putting the right information into your mind to make that decision to take back your life and be a "walking logo."

Conclusion

WHEN YOU LOOK at the Starts Within Organization's company logo, you will see a tale of two sides. You have a man on the left side wearing a prison uniform along with braids and a grimace on his face, guarding the prison bars. On the right side of the image, that same man wears a clean haircut, a suit, and an expression of contentment while guarding his family. It says that the story is about an individual going from being a liability in the community to becoming an asset through the decision to change his or her reality. So many people never get a chance to enter the right side of living and continue to stay stuck on the left, restricted by the prison bars.

You don't have to be in a facility to be in prison. You can be in prison within your own mind, and you will not move any farther, just as if you have bars stopping you. The only thing that can break the bars on our minds is the knowledge we obtain.

If people continue to live at a lower level after they have been exposed to the knowledge to do otherwise, then that is on them. If they haven't been exposed to the knowledge to live at a higher level, then that is on the people who possess the information and aren't doing everything they can to get it to the people who are thirsty for it.

The Walking Logo: Taking Back My Life gives people the information to live an enriched life that does not include prison. It discusses how to establish yourself in your children's lives through the courts or how to establish your finances by making good investments and establishing your credit. It is information that empowers you to properly manage your life so it can be all that it was created to be. We are created to live a life that is of quality and fulfilling, but until we make up our minds to do so, it will never happen.

I was twenty-nine years old when I got released from serving a ten-year prison sentence for attempted murder, possession of drugs, drug trafficking, and possession of firearms. I did not listen when everybody said the odds were stacked against me because of my background and that I would be back in prison within the first year of my release. Instead, I made my reality what I desired it to be, which was contradictory to what the statistics have stated. I have now been out of prison for ten years and twenty-three days, eclipsing my prison sentence by twenty-three days.

I got married, and I also got divorced. I have three children with three different women, but I have shared parenting in the courts with all my children, giving me the ability to establish a positive, uninterrupted relationship with them. I have been on family vacations, and I have been on exclusive brothers-only vacations to the Bahamas. I worked for minimum wage in a scrapyard in the worst conditions, but three years ago, I fired my boss and now do what I love for a living—help others duplicate the story of going from being a liability in the community to becoming an asset.

The Starts Within Organization that I cofounded in 2011 has been in existence for more than six years now, and we have created a program named the Walking Logo. This program enables us to go inside prisons and work with those who are getting released in eighteen to twenty-four months. We equip them with the information they need to avoid returning to prison upon release. I have found my mission, and you can tell it by the way I carry myself.

I truly believe the only thing stopping people from living a quality life is the information they receive that influences their thinking and controls their behavior, as I spoke about in my first published book, *Prison without Bars: It Starts Within*, which I wrote in 2015. Investing in people is the best investment you can make, because when people experience a better quality of living, it gives you the ability to experience a better quality of living as well.

Positive relationships are the most important assets you will have outside of time on this earth. Be sure to cherish and nurture those relationships; opportunity comes through them, and you can either get promoted to the

THE WALKING LOGO

next level of living or be stuck at the lower level, based solely on your relationships. Establish your positive relationship with God first, then yourself, and then with people, and your life will be grand! Your background and what you did will not be able to rob you of living on another level and being a true walking logo!

The Pledge of a Walking Logo

I am a Walking Logo who will learn how to soar to great heights in my life for the betterment of myself, my family, and those who are following me.

I am a person of character, commitment, and courage.

I am a person of integrity, intellect, and influence.

I am a person of discipline, determination, and dedication.

I am a person of faith, focus, and fortitude.

I am the designer of my own destiny; I challenge myself and others to be great.

I am successful in everything I do.

I am walking in love.

I am a magnet for success; I don't mistreat people.

I am my own walking life story; my life is governed by love, respect, and loyalty.

I am a Walking Logo. Not everyone has the right to speak into my life, and I will associate with family and friends who are ambassadors of truth and divine love.

I am built to succeed…I AM A WALKING LOGO.

CARLOS M. CHRISTIAN

Carlos M. Christian left prison after serving a ten-year sentence. He successfully transitioned back to society and now uses his journey as motivation for others. He has presented at the National Association for Blacks in Criminal Justice event "The Making of a Restored Citizen" and helped thousands of people make the transition through his company, the Starts Within Organization. His previous book, Prison without Bars, has been used in state penitentiaries and county jails throughout the United States.

Christian was the keynote speaker at the Restored Citizen Summit in Columbus, Ohio, and he was given the Ambassador for Fatherhood award by Action for Children because of his effectiveness in teaching thousands of fathers how to establish a positive relationship with their children.

The Walking Logo is his latest book.

THE WALKING LOGO

Brothers only Carnival Cruise to the Bahamas 2016.

CARLOS M. CHRISTIAN

Cleveland Browns scrimmage at The Ohio State with family 2016

THE WALKING LOGO

Changing the game by providing information that changes the mindsets of those who are incarcerated at Circleville Juvenile Correctional Facility

Enjoying our time in Miami riding in style 2017

THE WALKING LOGO

My two sons, daughter and, grandson. This is what an enriched life looks like!

CARLOS M. CHRISTIAN

Time well spent with my children!

THE WALKING LOGO

Mansfield Correctional Institution giving the men some energy in a full day workshop!

The 1995 Buick Regal in the background and Baby Bubba my middle child

THE WALKING LOGO

The 1995 Buick Regal has turned into the Benz I envisioned!

Made in the USA
Columbia, SC
26 March 2019